# STOCK TRADING AND INVESTING MADE EASY FOR BEGINNERS

Learn the basic foundations of how to be a successful trader and investor

By
Dr. Aderemi Banjoko

StockTrading4You Limited

*'Co-author in the # 1 Best selling Wake Up...Live the Life You Love book series'*

authorHOUSE®

*AuthorHouse™ UK Ltd.*
*500 Avebury Boulevard*
*Central Milton Keynes, MK9 2BE*
*www.authorhouse.co.uk*
*Phone: 08001974150*

*First published by AuthorHouse 3/30/2011*

*ISBN: 978-1-4520-1006-9 (sc)*
*ISBN: 978-1-4567-7668-8 (e)*

# Preface

I have always loved learning about different ways to create wealth. Straight out of medical school, I bought my first investment property in 1994 and I have not looked back since.

Along the way, I discovered the Stock Market and found it very interesting and fascinating. I loved the fact that it was a level playing field and anyone could get involved. I started trading and investing, read a lot of books and attended a lot of seminars. During this period, I discovered (after many huge losses!!!) that there were certain basic rules to trading and investing. Applying these rules to my trading and investing significantly improved my success.

I started to teach colleagues, friends and family on how to apply these rules which lead to me running seminars and courses on Stock Trading and Investing and now to writing this book.

I hope this book will give the beginner a good foundation to success in the Stock Market.

www.stocktrading4you.com

www.howtounderstandstockmarket.com

# Acknowledgments

First, I wish to give all honour and glory to God for giving me the ability to write this book and also to endure the good and bad experiences I have had during my career. I wish to especially thank my lovely wife, Mrs Helen Banjoko, for her understanding, support, patience and love which has been a great help during my career struggles and also completing this book.

www.stocktrading4you.com

www.howtounderstandstockmarket.com

www.stocktrading4you.com

www.howtounderstandstockmarket.com

"If you can actually count your money, then you are not really a rich man" – J. Paul Getty (1892 – 1976)

# Contents

# Introduction

## Benefits of Trading & Investing In the Financial Markets

As a Trader & Investor in the Stock Market, I have recognised many benefits in trading and investing. These are;

1. Being your own boss - You make your own decisions about which markets to trade or invest in and decide your own strategies.

2. You do not require any qualifications - Although you do need to learn the basics of trading and investing. You do not need to have a university degree to become a trader or investor. Continual self education on the financial markets, trading and investing is essential.

3. You can start with as little as £500 - Start small and with a good strategy and good money management, you can slowly build up your investment.

4. Earn unlimited amounts of money - There is no limit to how much you can earn on the stock market.

5. Trade and invest from anywhere in the world, hence you are not restricted and can make money on the move.

6. All you need is a laptop and internet access.

7. Everyone is equal in the Stock Market - The stock market respects no one and does not discriminate against anyone.

8. You can trade a variety of financial markets in different countries such as Indices, Foreign Exchange, Commodities, Individual stocks and shares.

9. You decide when or when not to trade and invest, making you the master of your time

10. You will gain a better understanding of the financial markets and the world economy.

These, along with other benefits, make me excited about being a Trader & Investor.

## The Difference Between Trading And Investing.

It is very important from the outset to understand that **trading** is significantly different from **investing**. Trading is **Short Term** and Investing is **Long Term**. With trading, you are looking to achieve your profit target within 24hours (Day Trading) or within a couple of weeks or couple of months (Swing Trading or Positional Trading).

With Investing, you are looking at a term of at least 10 – 20 years.

## Investing

Investing should be part of a core plan for building wealth. It involves putting small amounts of money on a regular basis into mutual funds, index funds, exchange traded funds (ETFs) etc.

The magic of compound interest is realised by this kind of investing, which magnifies small amounts invested over a period of time.

This money will be very useful towards retirement but ***not now***.

## Trading

Trading offers an opportunity to create good cash flow, once you have developed your mindset sufficiently and 'learned the rules of trading'. I will be discussing this further in the next chapter.

*'The greatest barrier to success is the fear of failure' – Sven Goran*

# Chapter 1

# Stock Trading Basics

Trading offers an opportunity to create good cash flow, once you have developed your mindset sufficiently and 'learned the rules of trading'.

Remember, trading may involve heavy losses, which can be minimised with a strong development of your mindset.

To become a successful trader in the stock market, you must possess what I call the **three 'M's, M**ind, **M**oney Management and **M**ethod.

## Mind

A disciplined mind is an absolute requirement for successful trading. Managing to conquer the devils of greed and fear will enable you to become a successful trader. Greed could make you take unnecessary risks leading to HUGE losses. Fear may paralyse you and stop you from placing trades which leads to losing out on potentially profitable trades.

Learn to manage your emotions. Your success or failure as a trader is largely due to your ability to control your emotions and maintain your discipline.

***Your Goal should be to trade well and not to make money!*** If you trade well, you will make money.

## Money Management

This is another important factor in trading. The *first* goal of money management is *survival!* You need to avoid risk that can put you out of business. The *second* goal is to earn a steady return and the *third* is to continue to improve on the second goal.

Taking into consideration your capital investment, managing your risk per trade is extremely crucial to your success in becoming a profitable trader.

## Method

There needs to be a plan or methodology to trading which is not based on tips, hunches, visions or dreams. Developing a personalised trading plan is essential as without a trading plan, you are setting yourself up for failure.

*It is not only important to have a trading plan, you have to be disciplined and stick to it!*

You need to remember that trading in the correct way, with the 3 'M's in mind will make you money. If your target is just to earn money instead of trading in the proper way, this may lead to the loss of huge sums of money. The 3 'M's will be discussed in more detail in the subsequent chapters.

## Opening a Trading Account

It is now very easy to open a trading account and there are a lot of online trading brokerage firms out there.

*It is very important as a beginner to have a mentor guide you through placing you first trades, setting up your trading platform and helping you with understanding how to analyse the financial markets.*

Here are a few online brokerage firms which you may find useful.

➤ www.cmcmarkets.com

- ➢ www.igindex.co.uk

- ➢ www.optionsxpress.com

*Always remember, the financial markets are dynamic with real people buying and selling for various reasons which may be logical or illogical. Hence the financial markets do not always follow what the text books or analysts say. Avoid using the words ALWAYS and NEVER when analysing the markets.*

*'Knowing is not enough, we must apply. Willing is not enough, we must do' – Goethe*

# Chapter 2

# Mind (Psychology of Trading) and Money Management

## Mind (Psychology of Trading)

This happens to be the most important aspect of trading. A large part of your success is down to you and your discipline!! In order to be a successful trader, you need to master your mind and trading psychology.

Here are a few ways to help you understand trading psychology.

1. **Learn to manage your emotions.**

   You need to be objective and clear in your mind when assessing the financial markets. If you are upset, excited, tired, and angry or distracted for any reason, you should not be trading. Your feelings have an immediate impact on your account.

2. **Do not ignore change in mass psychology.**

   The trend in the market is a reflection of what the majority of the traders in the market think. If the majority of traders in the market are buying, the market and trend will go up but if the majority of traders decide to sell, the direction of the market can change and start to trend downwards. This means you should be willing to change your mind once you notice a change in the direction of the market. Ignoring change in mass psychology can result in huge losses. It pays to remember the old saying *'The Trend is Your Friend'*.

You need to be humble as a trader and be willing to change your mind. Huge losses may occur if you become arrogant and refuse to change your mind when the markets are moving against you.

### 3.  Trade less often.

Every trade you place is a potentially losing trade, hence the more trades you place the greater the risk of losing a lot of money. Usually the biggest mistake new traders make is to think the more trades they place, the more successful they will be.

### 4.  Trading is deceptively easy.

Being successful in your first few trades can lead to the notion that trading is easy. Huge losses may result because the trader can become over confident, greedy, and not aware of the other factors that come into play with trading such as fundamental analysis, economic news, chart patterns and the previous history of the market.

### 5.  The Goal is to trade well and not to make money.

If you trade well, you will make money. My advice to new traders is to focus on how to properly analyse the financial markets, how to formulate a trading plan, how to develop their mind, good discipline and how to apply good money management to their trades.

Focusing solely on profits and making money leads to poor decision making, greed, over trading, poor money management and lack of discipline which could all lead to huge losses.

6. **You are responsible for your trades.**

Learning to take responsibility for your trades will help you learn from your bad trades and help improve your trading. Blaming the news, friends, your broker, your mentor or anyone and anything around you for your bad trades will prevent you learning from these bad trades and doomed to repeating the same mistakes again.

It is also a good idea to keep a diary of your trades. Continuous analysis of your trades and yourself aids the development of a successful trading career. Importantly, keeping reading, attending seminars and learning about the financial markets and trading.

7. **Beware there are enormous temptations in the market.**

The markets can be highly volatile with sudden changes in direction. Without a good trading plan and discipline, this could lead to emotionally driven trades resulting in huge losses.

8. **Rags to riches and riches to rags stories.**

Applying the basics of trading well, (the 3 'Ms'), could create a rags to riches story. Indiscipline, failure to plan and not applying the 3 'Ms' could lead to riches to rags stories.

9. **Formulate a trading plan.**

Write down your trading plan and stick to it. Plan your trades and trade your plan! See chapter 6 on Trading Plan.

10. **Strict Money Management rules.**

# Money Management

This is the most critical, yet frequently overlooked, aspect associated with trading. Irrespective of which financial market you are trading, what trading program or strategy an individual is using or whether the market is up or down, without excellent money management you will not succeed in turning out to be a profitable trader.

Using excellent money management, you can end up being successful with a winning percentage of less than 50% of trades.

A good article, titled 'Why It's So Difficult for Most People to Make Money in the Market', written by Dr. Van K. Tharp in the November 1997 newsletter of the Market Technicians Association, he states that, 'Most of us grew up exposed to an educational system that brainwashes us with the idea that you have to get 94-95% correct to be excellent. And if you can't get at least 70% correct you're a failure. Mistakes are severely punished in the school system by ridicule and poor grades, yet it is only through mistakes that human beings learn. Contrast that with the real world in which a .300 hitter in baseball gets paid millions. In fact, in the everyday world few people are close to perfect and most of us who do well are probably right less than half the time. Indeed, people have made millions on trading systems with reliabilities around 40%'.

Gerald Loeb wrote, in The Battle for Investment Survival, that "The most important single thing I learned is that accepting losses promptly is the first key to success." Loeb goes on to say, "The difference between the investor who year in and year out procures for himself a final net profit and the one who is usually in the red is not entirely a question of superior selection of stocks or superior timing. Rather, it is also a case of knowing how to capitalize successes and curtail failures."

Your ultimate objective of accomplishing profitability will remain out of reach except if good care is actually taken in order to control the amount of capital allocated to each position, as even wildly successful traders are not invulnerable to a string of losing positions.

Goals of money management are in the following rank of priority

1st – Long term survival!

2nd – Steady growth of capital

3rd – High profits

Winners think, feel and act differently from losers. You might have to change your personality.

## Tips to Successful Trading

1.  Decide you are in the market for the long haul i.e. 20+ years. This is not a get rich quick scheme. Focus on managing your risks and not on your profits. Learn to live to trade another day by not taking undue risks and jeopardising your entire capital in one day!

2.  Learn as much as you can from books, seminars, and experts but be sceptical. Continual education is very important in becoming a good trader.

3.  Do not get greedy and rush to trade – learn to trade properly.

4.  Develop a method of analysing the market

5.  Be aware, traders could be the weakest link in trading.

*'It is hard to fail, but it is worse never to have tried to succeed' - Theodore Roosevelt*

# Chapter 3

# Fundamental Analysis & Intermarket Analysis

## Fundamental Analysis (FA)

### Definition of Fundamental Analysis (FA)

This is the examination involving any main factors which influence the state of the economy, industry groups and companies.

The goal is usually to derive a prediction and then benefit from future price movements.

FA is actually performed on 3 levels, starting typically through the economic level, then the industry sector level as well as finally the company level.

### National Economy Stage

You should focus on economic data to analyse the existing as well as long term growth of the particular economy.

Whenever the economy grows, industry groups and companies benefit and also expand.

When the overall economy shrinks or declines, most sectors as well as companies are affected.

Generally there are several economic reports to be aware of which impact the economy such as Interest Rates, Gross Domestic Product, Consumer Price Index and Nonfarm Payrolls (Unemployment figures) to name a few.

## Industry Stage

This involves you examining the actual supply and demand forces pertaining to the products and services of the industry sector you are interested in.

Generally, you identify industry sectors which usually profit the most out of growth of the economy and the industry sectors that are usually affected the least from the downfall associated with the economy.

It is much more beneficial to choose to be in the right industry sector than with the correct stock.

You will need to search to find the Leaders & Innovators within the industry group.

## Company Stage

This requires you to actually assess the financial data, management, organization concept as well as levels of competition relating to the company you are interested in.

Deriving current good value and forecasting foreseeable future stock prices requires analysis involving all 3 levels.

## Advantages of Fundamental Analysis Include;

➢ A good decision making tool for long-term investments based on long-term trends.

➢ The identification of valuable stocks.

➢ A development of a thorough understanding of the business.

# Disadvantages of Fundamental Analysis are;

➢ Time constraints – to adequately fundamentally analyse the markets consumes time.

➢ It is heavily based on subjectivity – A fair value of a stock is based on assumptions

➢ Analyst bias – The majority of the information that goes into the analysis comes from the company itself.

# Intermarket Analysis

Structural shifts involving economic markets have arisen because the global economy has emerged due to innovations within telecommunications as well as escalating internationalization associated with business and also commerce.

Hardly any economy will be isolated in the current world financial system.

It is important to factor into your analysis, outside intermarket forces that impact each market traded.

Most of the commodities industry carries an impact on the Treasury notes and Bonds. This has a strong impact on the equities market, which in turn has a strong impact on the price of the US dollar as well as foreign exchange markets which subsequently has a great influence upon commodities and the cycle continues.

In addition, the United States economy makes an impact on the world's market segments and the world's markets present an impact on the US economy.

*Always remember, the financial markets are dynamic with real people buying and selling for various reasons which may be logical or illogical. Hence the financial markets do not always follow what*

*the text books or analysts say. Avoid using the words ALWAYS and NEVER when analysing the markets.*

## Gold, Oil & Foreign Exchange

If the actual worth of the US dollar drops, gold prices rise. US dollar and gold usually go in opposite directions.

You can find some sort of positive correlation between Euro and gold. The actual value associated with Euro and gold prices frequently move in the same direction.

Oil is currently an important commodity driving worldwide economic growth. Oil prices and foreign exchange possess an important association in the global economy.

Raised oil prices weakens the Yen and strengthens the value of the pound sterling.

## Agricultural Commodities

Exports associated with agricultural commodities account for a sizable portion of USA farm revenue.

Whenever the value for dollar rises, this cuts down interest coming from importing nations because of the commodity's inflated costs and as a result there is a downfall within the commodity market.

If the value of dollar drops, commodity prices become cheap and the market goes up.

*'Energy and persistence conquer all things' – Benjamin Franklin*

# Chapter 4

# Technical Analysis & Indicators

**Various definitions of Technical Analysis describe this as;**

1. A technique of reviewing the market activity (Currency trading, commodities, stocks and shares and indices), patterns on any graph and or chart in order to discover buying and selling possibilities.

2. A visual representation regarding price and volume movements through time frame

3. The predicting of market prices through methods of study from information created through the course of stock trading. For example, while trading a stock you might notice price patterns indicating a rise in the stock price giving you an indication to buy the stock.

Technical analysis is not solely effective to the short-term or intermediate-term trader, but also helps the long-term investor as well.

In order to be a good trader, knowledge of how to examine a stock chart is crucial. Failure to assess, figure out and interpret the charts of the markets you are trading makes you greatly handicapped. Reading books in addition to articles on technical analysis and continual education is very important in becoming a successful trader.

Technical analysis will **not** predict the foreseeable future, however it will provide a guide within which to analyze the market and come up with reasonable options to trade.

One of the most important goals associated with graph and or chart study is to verify the trend associated with the market. A very good old and popular statement within stock trading is 'The Trend is Your Friend'. The trend is the observable course associated with the market which could be up, down or sideways. Trading in the direction associated with the trend can substantially boosts your chances of success.

## Indicators

This means any kind of numerical calculation that is displayed graphically upon the graph and or chart other than **time** and **price**.

Indicators facilitate the analysis of the markets. Be very careful not to make use of too many indicators on your graph or chart as this could lead to confusion and even hamper your trading. It is better to make use of 2or a maximum of 3 indicators on a chart.

Indicators are mainly used to decide entry and exit points in the markets.

## Types of Indicators

There are many indicators used in trading and it is outside the scope of this book to explain the different indicators and how to use them. A few examples of how to use them can be found in Chapter 7 on Trading Strategies. I recommend you read up and study the individual indicators you choose to trade with.

A few of the frequently used indicators are;

- ➢ Candlesticks
- ➢ Trend lines
- ➢ Support & Resistance

- ➢ Moving averages (MA)

- ➢ Pivot points

- ➢ Volume

- ➢ Fibonacci retracement

- ➢ MACD – Moving Average Convergence Divergence

*'Only through experiences of trial and suffering can the soul be strengthened' – Helen Keller*

# Chapter 5

# Method of Trading – Trading Plan

**Here are Four Important Reasons to have a Trading Plan**

1. A Trading Plan helps you plan your trades – Adopting a method or strategy with which you use to trade is very important otherwise you are frankly gambling and not trading.

2. It makes you consistent – Having a plan minimises guess work and improves consistency your trades. This helps you become a successful trader.

3. Objectivity – Having a plan enhances the analysis of your trading strategy and trading history in an objective way because you have been applying a consistent plan. This aids your assessment in an objective way whether your plan is successful or not.

4. To establish discipline – This is a way of keeping yourself in check and avoiding outside interference with your trading. It is also a way of assessing yourself as to whether *you (perhaps your feelings and emotions)* are the cause of your bad trades or the plan *(Checks if you are applying the '3'M to your trading!!)*.

A trading method or strategy, consistency, objectivity and discipline make the components of a good trader.

# Simple Features of a Trading Plan should;

- ➢ State which markets you wish to trade

- ➢ State which time frame in which you wish to trade for the chosen market

- ➢ Have strict criteria for market entry – identifying which indicators to use

- ➢ Set strict criteria for market exit – when profit target has been reached and more importantly, when loss limit has also been reached to exit market.

**An Example of a simple trading plan for illustration purposes only**

- ➢ Market to Trade – Forex - EUR/USD

- ➢ Trade contract size – 1/point (£1 per point)

- ➢ Use *risk* (how many points you are willing to lose if the market goes against you) to *reward* (how many points you plan to make if the market moves in your direction) ratio of 1:3 (Day Trading)

- ➢ Use a *stop loss* (set a limit of how many points you are willing to lose if the market goes against you) of 20points and *Profit Limit* (set a limit of how many points you want to make if the market moves in your direction) of 60points (Day Trading)

- ➢ Swing Trading – Use a stop loss of 100points and Profit taking (exit) at next Fibonacci retracement.

- ➢ Always check the economic calendar for reports of HIGH importance before you commence trading for the day.

- ➢ Do not trade before a report of high importance comes out.

- Check the 1year Daily chart first for an overview of the market.

- For Swing Trades I use the Fibonacci Retracements as my entry and exit points.

- For Day trading – Use the 2days 5mins Chart and Pivot Points for points of entry into the market.

- Use the Moving Average 50 (MA50) as the trend indicator and only trade in the direction of the trend.

- When the market is trending sideways, DO NOT TRADE!

- When I have 3 consecutive losses, STOP TRADING FOR THE DAY!!!!

- When profit target has been achieved, STOP TRADING FOR THE DAY!!!!

'The most efficient way of spending money is to spend you own, and the least efficient way is to spend other people's' – Milton Friedman

# Chapter 6

# Markets to Trade

Another trading plan aspect to consider will be the markets you trade. There are lots of diverse markets with plenty of liquidity to allow for sensible speculation. Having said that, it is important to select markets that are appropriate for your account size, risk level and trading style.

Trading with a good varied portfolio gives you a greater chance of capturing some of the really significant moves that make for successful trading.

In this particular chapter, the Indices Market (Index) and Foreign Exchange Market (FOREX) will be discussed.

## Indices (Index)

Indices are one of the markets you can add to your portfolio.

### Stock Exchange Index

A market index is a technique of calculating a piece of the particular exchange of a nation. The most regularly quoted market indices tend to be broad-base indices consisting of the stocks and shares of large companies mentioned on a nation's main stock exchanges, such as,

FTSE 100 Index - Measures the United Kingdom Stock Exchange

DJ 30 & SP 500 Index - Measures the United States Stock Exchange

DAX 30 Index - Measures the Stock Exchange in Germany

Aussie 200 Index - Measures the Stock Exchange in Australia

CAC 40 Index - Measures the Stock Exchange in France

# Weighting

This involves the whole market capitalization of the companies weighted by their effect on the particular index, so that the bigger stocks will make much more of a change in the index when compared with a smaller market cap company.

Price-weighted index - such as the FTSE 100, the cost of each component stock will be the sole factor when ever determining the value of the index.

Market-value weighted or capitalization-weighted index like the Hang Seng Index factors in the size of the company.

Innovative methods of index structure will probably overtake conventional market capitalisation-weighted indices as being the dominant factor of equity baselines within 20years, according to FTSE Group.

A number of alternative methods have surfaced lately, such as Fundamental Indices by which stocks are weighted by metrics like book value, dividends and sales and Minimum Variance, by which portfolios are designed to minimize volatility.

# FTSE ( Financial Times Stock Exchange ) 100

This is a share index using the hundred most significantly capitalised United Kingdom firms listed on the London Stock Exchange. The index launched on 3 January 1984 with a base level of 1000, the top worth reached so far is 6950.6, on 30 December 1999.

The index is managed by the FTSE Group, an independent company which originated as a collaboration involving the financial times *(FT)* and the London Stock Exchange *(SE)*. It is usually figured out in real-time and released every 15 seconds.

FTSE 100 companies represent about 81% of the market capitalisation of the entire London Stock Exchange. Although the FTSE All-Share Index is much more comprehensive, the FTSE 100 is by far the most commonly used UK stock market indicator.

## Factors Which Usually Affect Indices

- National economic data.
- Company data.
- Time of the year – Common saying is 'Buy in November & Sell in April'.

## Market Opening Times

- FTSE 100 - 8am - 4.30pm GMT london
- Dow Jones - 9.30am - 4pm ET
- Aussie 200 - 10.00am - 4pm AEST

## Foreign Exchange - FOREX

## Advantages of FOREX Trading

- Diversification – Huge variety of currency pairs to trade.
- Global Market and 24 Hour Trading
- Liquidity - The forex market stands out as the largest and the most liquid among the world's financial market. More than $4 trillion is usually traded a day within the forex market.
- Leverage – Forex is usually traded on leverage.

- Good Technical Market – Due to the huge volume involved in the forex market, it is a good market for technical analysis.

As a result, forex is an important inclusion to a trader's portfolio

Forex consists of trading one kind of currency for another in what is known as currency pairs. Forex is actually a two-dimensional product.

## History

There is no central exchange with regard to the forex market. It operates through a worldwide network of banking institutions, organizations as well as individuals trading one currency for another.

The forex market was initially created to facilitate trade among countries.

Today a large portion of the forex market is traded on speculation, arbitrage and professional dealing.

The Bretton Woods Agreement (1944 – 1971) pegged dollar to gold at a price of $35 an ounce.

Richard Nixon, on August 15, 1971, removed the US from the "gold standard". This lead to the Smithsonian Agreement in December 1971.

With this and the advent of computers, technology and the internet, the forex market blossomed to what it has become today.

## Currency Pair

Forex is a 2-dimensional product. It is quoted as the price of one currency against another.

The base currency is always quoted first and this has a constant of 1. The base currency is what you are buying or selling.

For example, EUR/USD - 1.2619, means 1 Euro (base currency) is equivalent to 1.2619 US Dollars.

## Factors that affect the Forex Market

- US Non-Farm Payrolls – US unemployment report.
- Interest Rate decisions
- Gross Domestic Product (GDP)
- Consumer Price Index (CPI)
- US Federal Open Market Committee (FOMC) Meetings

*'Failure is the opportunity to begin again more intelligently' – Henry Ford*

# Chapter 7

# Trading Strategies

Trading strategies are an important aspect of your trading plan. This involves deciding what criteria and indicators you will use to determine your entry point into the market as well as an exit strategy.

You will also need to decide whether you are swing trading or day trading.

A **Day Trader** is looking to achieve profit targets within 24hours and a **Swing Trader** is looking to achieve profit targets within several days or sometimes several weeks.

**In summary**

> ➢ Decide which technical indicators to use. Try to use only two, maximum three, indicators when trading.

> ➢ Clearly define your entry & exit criteria.

> ➢ STICK TO YOUR PLAN AND BE CONSISTENT!

There are as many strategies as there are traders that can be used for Swing Trading and Day Trading. It is advisable to attend seminars and lectures on trading and also seek the guidance of a mentor on how to use these or other strategies in trading and most importantly to help you formulate your own trading strategy.

***It is very important to remember that no trading strategy will give you a 100% success rate!!***

It will be a futile attempt to look for the perfect trading strategy. You can be a very successful trader with a winning percentage of 40% of trades (see money management in Chapter 3).

**Here are a few examples of trading strategies.**

**Swing Trading**

- Using the **Fibonacci Retracements** on the 1year Daily chart time frame – As entry and exit points. See chart below.

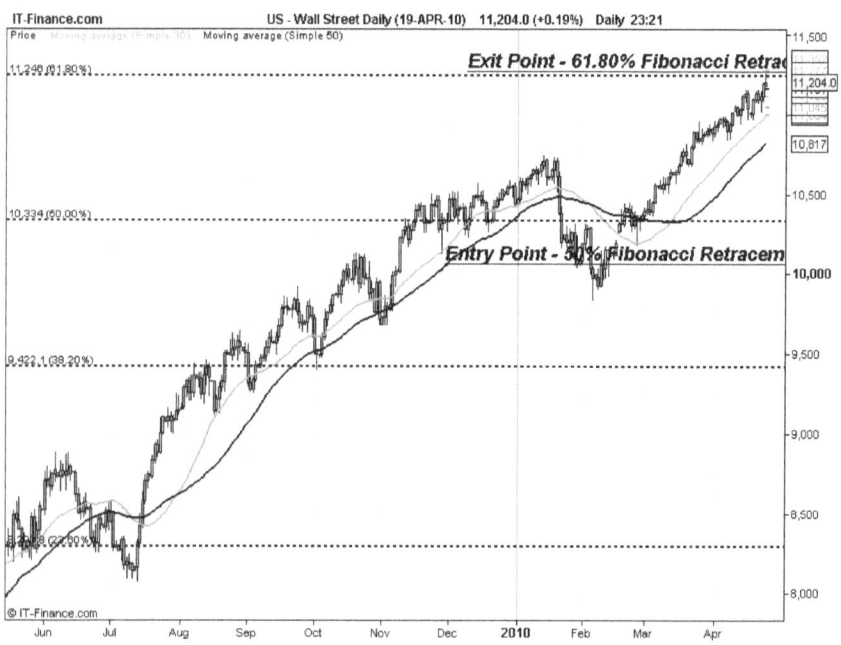

- Using the **Moving Averages (MA)** - MA50 (Black line) & MA30 (Red line) on the 1year Daily chart time frame – As entry and exit points. See chart below.

## Day Trading

- Using **Pivot points** (Broken horizontal lines) on the 2Day 5Minutes chart time frame – As entry and exit points. See chart below.

- **Support & Resistance** – Identifying the support and resistance levels in the markets and trading the breakouts from a sideways trend. See chart below.

*'Always bear in mind that your own resolution to success is more important than any other one thing'* – *Abraham Lincoln*

# Chapter 8

# Long Term Investment in the Stock Market

## What is the foundation to Long Term Investing?

To emerge as a successful long term investor, you need to develop these four crucial financial skills;

1. How to appreciate the value of money

2. How to Control Money

3. Actively implement effective ways to help you save Money

4. And finally, ways to Invest Money

## How to appreciate the value of money

Investing just £30 a month can generate a Million pounds (£1Million) by way of the influence of compound interest. The dictionary definition of compound interest is; 'interest paid on both the principal (capital) and on accrued interest'.

Wealthy individuals *gain* compound interest while poor individuals *pay* compound interest.

During my early years in business, I often had more credit cards and personal loan debts than income from my businesses. I soon realized that despite payments to loan companies, the outstanding debt was more or less the same. It is important to make your money to work for you than you to work for money!! I started looking for investments and businesses that earned me compound interest and became mindful of what I spent my money on.

Using a compound interest calculator, below is a table showing how long it will take to generate a million pounds on saving £30 per month, depending on the interest rate.

| Interest Rate | Time in Years on Saving £30 per month |
|---|---|
| 5% | 101 |
| 10% | 59 |
| 15% | 43 |
| 20% | 35 |

There are different ways to look at this table. First and foremost, you need to find the money to invest. If you want to shorten the duration, you will need to invest more. Think about what you are currently spending your money on and whether you are spending wisely and investing wisely.

The other point to note from this table is the importance of starting early when it comes to investing for our children's future.

## How to manage and also save Money

It is very important to record all your income and expenses. Poor record keeping of my income and expenses was a major reason for my earlier failures in business. With a very clear view of your financial situation, you will be able to see where you are losing money and where you might save money.

Once you have a clear picture of your finances, save at least 6-9months of emergency money in order for you to cover your expenses for 6-9months in the event of job loss of collapse of business.

From then on, 50% from your savings go straight to your Long term investment account.

See Appendix 1 for an example of a simple income and expenses spreadsheet you can use.

# Long Term Money Investment

This enables investors to gain from wealth generation and the growth associated with a nation's economy. This is done by finding a way to invest in the Stock Market of a country you are interested in.

Hence the first decision to make in Long Term Investing is which country *you think* is going to generate wealth and economic growth in the next 10-20years.

You can choose to make investments in stocks & shares of companies, mutual funds, index funds, Exchange Traded Funds (ETFs), cash, bonds and so on in the country of your choice.

You do not necessarily need to learn everything regarding these types of passive financial instruments, but you should be aware of the essential basics.

# The Basics of Long Term Investing

There are 3 main methods for investors to gain access to the stock market.

1. **Invest directly in Stocks & Shares**

   There are more than 10,000 stocks to choose from in the United Kingdom alone. This form of investment requires a good knowledge of the company you are interested in. You should get to know the products or services of the company, the competition, future plans, management board and other relevant details of the company. You also have to know how to read company financials and understand Price/Earnings (P/E) ratios (a valuation ratio of a company's current share price compared to its per-share earnings), Earnings Per Share (EPS) (The portion of a company's profit allocated to each outstanding share of common stock) and other terms involved in the understanding of company financials.

All this is time consuming but good knowledge and experience will provide you with the ability to pick good stocks. Warren Buffet is the greatest stock picker in the world.

A full and comprehensive discussion on how to pick good stocks to invest in long term is outside the scope of this book and this is a method of Long Term Investing that beginners will need to approach with extreme caution.

2. **Investments in Actively Managed Funds – Mutual Funds**

A mutual fund is a professionally managed type of collective investment scheme that pools money from many investors and invests in stocks and shares and other financial instruments. The mutual fund will have a fund manager that buys and sells the fund's investments in accordance with the fund's investment objective.

There are mutual funds that invest in stocks and shares of companies called *Equity Funds*. Mutual funds that invest in bonds are called *Fixed -Income Funds* and mutual funds that invest in the money market are known as a *Money Market Fund*.

Basically, you are getting someone else to pick the companies and stocks on your behalf in exchange for a management fee payment.

The benchmark for most mutual funds is the index of the country where the fund is invested. A nation's index represents the performance of the stock market of a given nation and this usually reflects investor sentiment on the state of its economy. The index in the United Kingdom (UK) is called the FTSE 100 and is composed of the top 100 large capitalized companies in UK. In the United States of America (USA), the index is the Dow Jones 30 (top 30 companies) or the Standard & Poor (S&P) 500 (the top 500 companies).

Many fund managers attempt to achieve better returns than the FTSE 100 in UK or the S&P 500 in the United States and are largely unsuccessful.

3. **Invest in Passively Managed Funds**

Index funds and Exchange Traded Funds are passively managed funds as explained below.

**An Index fund** is a portfolio constructed to match or track the components of a market index, such as the FTSE 100 in UK or the Standard & Poor's 500 Index (S&P 500) in USA. An index fund provides broad market exposure hence spreading and reducing the risk.

**An Exchange Traded Fund (ETF)** is a security that tracks an index, a commodity or a basket of assets like an index fund, but trades like a stock on an exchange. ETFs experience price changes throughout the day as they are bought and sold.

These funds are passively managed leading to low operating expenses.

Since most fund managers are trying to beat the returns of the index, if you cannot beat them, join them – buy index funds or ETFs. Index funds and ETFs can be a safer option for beginner investors to start with.

To find Mutual funds, Index funds or ETFs to invest in, you may find www.morningstar.com helpful. You may also want to open an investment account and check for these funds with brokers such as Hargreaves Lansdown at www.h-l.co.uk, Fidelity at www.fidelity.co.uk (UK) or www.fidelity.com (USA). These sites are a few of many options.

## Important checks when evaluating funds

1.  **Total Expense Ratio (TER)** – these are fees charged towards management costs and other services of running the fund. This affects the actual returns you receive on the fund. For example, if a fund has a return of 20% and the TER is 3% your actual return is 17%.

    Funds with a higher turnover, usually Mutual Funds, have a high TER whereas funds with a low turnover, usually index funds or ETFs, have a low TER, as low as 0 – 0.3%.

2.  **Whether to opt In or Out of an ISA** (Individual Savings Allowance) – Investment or savings in an ISA is *tax free* in the UK. From aged 18years and above, you can contribute up to £10,200 a year (£850 per month) into your ISA account. It is important to check you can invest the fund in an ISA account and maximise your allowance before investing over of an ISA.

    There are also investment pension accounts that can be opened which are tax efficient such as the Self Invested Personal Pensions (SIPP) in the UK or the Individual Retirement Account (IRA) in the USA.

    Consult an investment account broker for further details of these retirement accounts.

3.  **5-10 year Performance of the fund** – This gives you a good long term picture of the performance of the fund compared to a very short history of 1-2years. If a fund is doing well over a 5 – 10year period, it could be assessed as showing good

management and a good strategy for that fund. However there are **NO** guarantees for the future returns of the funds but it is better to choose a fund with a good long history with speculated prospects of a good future.

## Taking Action with Long Term Investment

**When to invest?** – Start investing as soon as you can and practice dollar cost averaging and benefit from compound interest.

Dollar Cost Averaging - This involves buying a fixed dollar amount of a particular investment on a regular schedule (such as monthly), regardless of the share price. More shares or units are purchased when prices are low, and fewer shares are bought when prices are high. This is a sophisticated way of investing.

**When to Sell?** - The longer you invest, the lower the risk. Look at 10-20years.

## Summary
### 7 Steps to Long Term Investing

1. Get your finances in order and determine how much you can comfortably afford to invest on a monthly basis in order to benefit from compound interest and dollar cost averaging.

2. Determine which country, industry sector or commodity you feel will benefit from long term growth.

3. First look for index funds or ETFs which track the countries index, industry sector or commodities of your choice. If you cannot find index funds or ETFs to track the markets of your choice, you can then look at mutual funds.

4. Check the TER, the 5-10 year performance and whether you can invest these funds in tax efficient vehicles such as ISAs, SIPPs or IRA.

5. Open an Investment Account with an investment broker of your choice.

6. Discuss your investment objectives and obtain financial advice from your financial adviser.

7. Decide how you want to allocate your monthly investment. See Asset Allocation in next chapter.

*The soul of a lazy man desires and has nothing; But the soul of the diligent shall be rich – Proverbs 13v4 (NKJV).*

# Chapter 9

## Asset Allocation

This is the method of widening your investments across a variety of different asset sectors and geographical regions.

Asset allocation helps to reduce the chance of **all** your investments falling in worth at the same time and maximises the potential for smoother, and so higher compound returns. This is the most efficient method in reducing risk when the assets selected rise and fall in worth independently of one another, that is, their movements in prices are not associated.

Asset allocation can effectively diversify the portfolio of an investor in one of two ways.

1. Through the addition of assets to your portfolio which are not related to stocks and shares. As an example, adding gold, commodities, and bonds to your portfolio of shares is known as **vertical** diversification.

2. Through the addition of stocks and shares assets only from other geographical regions (such as UK, USA & Europe) or other sectors (such as financial, oil and gas or retail sector) is known as **horizontal** diversification.

# Ways of Allocating Assets

1. You can strategically place your assets by allocating a fixed percentage of your capital investment to your different investments. For instance, a straightforward strategic allocation for a twenty year term could be fifty percent stocks & shares, twenty-five percent bonds, fifteen percent property and ten percent commodities.

2. To exploit transient commercial or market conditions and augment returns, you can temporarily deviate from the strategic asset allocation above and revert back when you have achieved your profits. This form of tactical asset allocation requires good knowledge of the market and good market timing.

3. The upkeep of the same portfolio weighting to each asset group, irrespective of which assets are rising or falling in value is termed the constant-weighting asset allocation. For instance, if the commodities portion rose in price from ten percent to twenty percent of the portfolio, commodities would be sold and other assets purchased to revive the weighting.

# When to Assess & Modify Your Portfolio of Investments

Asset allocation could need to be modified over time, for 2 reasons:

1. Increase in volatility of the portfolio due to rises in the value of the assets and changing market conditions. This assessment does not have to be done every day. Every 3 – 6months is sufficient and this is the beauty of long term investment.

2. An individual's age can lower the risk toleration of an investor, particularly in the years before retirement. The younger you are the more aggressive you can be with your investments and a large portion of your portfolio can consist of financial instruments such as equities (stocks and shares) and commodities. The

closer you are to retirement age, the more cautious you should be and you might want to consider allocating a large portion of your portfolio to safer investments like bonds, treasury bills and cash.

## Achieving Asset Allocation

Investors can now achieve nearly any asset allocation by holding a straightforward portfolio of low cost index tracking exchange-traded funds (ETFs). There are a wide range of ETFs to choose from and they can track the index, different sectors and also commodities.

Different types of ETFs could be found using websites such as www.morningstar.co.uk (UK) or www.morningstar.com (USA). You can also check and analyse ETFs through your investment broker's website.

## Exchange Traded Funds (ETFs)

Index tracker funds, which track stock market indices, were thought to be the best thing when they were first launched in the UK in 1988.

But since 2000, index tracker funds have had a competitor in the form of exchange traded funds which can similarly mirror market indices, but via a share, rather than a fund.

However, despite having several advantages over index tracker funds, ETFs have been relatively slow to take off in the UK retail investment market.

ETFs are shares that are traded on a stock exchange and whose assets mirror the price movements of the underlying share portfolio of an index, sector or commodity, such as the FTSE 100, financial sector shares or gold.

In 2006, the European ETF sector grew by 50 per cent to almost £50bn, and is now growing more quickly than the well established US ETF market, which is already worth $600bn.

Index Funds and ETFs are similar in that they both aim to mirror an underlying index, but the difference is that an ETF is a share which can be traded at any time of the trading day, whereas an index tracker fund is a unit trust which can only be traded at one point in the trading day.

# APPENDIX

1. Income and Expenses Spreadsheet

## Resources and Events

### Membership Program

Join the membership program and benefit from regular webinars on stock trading and investing, mentorship and online live trading sessions. Details of how to join can be found on the website at www.stocktrading4you.com.

### Stock Trading Seminars & Weekend Wealth Retreats

Attend live stock trading seminars and learn how to trade the financial markets including forex trading, indices and options trading.

Attend the weekend wealth retreat and benefit from in-depth teaching on the Stock Market and other income streams such as Real Estate and Internet Marketing.

Further details can be found at the website, www.stocktrading4you.com, at the events section.

### Regular tutorials on the Stock Market

You can also subscribe to receive regular tutorials including video tutorials on Understanding The Stock Market at www. howtounderstandstockmarket.com.

### Forex Day Trading Blog and StockTrading4You Channel

Follow my forex day and swing trades on my blog at www. forexdaytrading4you.blogspot.com and on youtube at www.youtube. com/user/StockTrading4You

### Recorded Webinars on Various Streams of Income

Watch recorded webinars on various income streams from guest speakers at www.enlightenedwealthcreation.blogspot.com.

*'Risk comes from not knowing what you're doing' – Warren Buffett*

# Back Page

Most people I meet tend to either think the Stock Market is complex and difficult or that it is easy to make money on the Stock Market. I fell into the category of thinking the Stock Market was easy but I soon found out that there are rules to trading and if applied correctly, could lead to profitable trading and investing.

I have since taught people how to trade and invest wisely and dispel the many myths surrounding the Stock Market.

This book on Stock Trading & Investing for Beginners has been published to give the reader an essential foundation as they venture into the exciting world of Trading & Investing.

Dr. Aderemi Banjoko is a fully registered medical practitioner with the General Medical Council in the United Kingdom. He has a keen interest in Stock Market Trading & Investing. The experience and knowledge gained was largely due to learning from expensive mistakes, which he hopes to prevent others making the same mistakes. He runs stock trading and investment seminars and also online training, details of which can be found at www.stocktrading4you.com. You can also follow him on twitter at www.twitter.com/stocktrading4.

He is passionate about his charity work with orphans and widows and hopes to encourage more people to give their time, efforts and money in helping less fortunate individuals.